CONTENTS

Decorating Guide

Snowball Mountain Challenge: Find Your Strength in God

	Bible Story	Lift Lessons	Music	Crafts
Session 1	Joseph Interprets Dreams (Genesis 40:1–41:45)	I can share my gifts!	• Snowball Mountain Challenge • Philippians 4:13 • I've Got a Gift • Snowball Mountain Day	• Mosaic Snowflake • Kaleidoscope • Chalet • Fan
Session 2	Esther Shows Courage (Esther 3:7–8:8)	I can be brave!	• I've Got a Gift • Snowball Mountain Challenge • C-O-U-R-A-G-E • Snowball Mountain Day	• Watercolor Mountain • Seal Paper Doll • Twirl Toy
Session 3	The Widow's Offering (Mark 12:41-44)	I can give my all!	• Philippians 4:13 • Anything But You • Supersized • Snowball Mountain Challenge	• Air Clay Snow Challenger • Upcycle Prayer Box • Coin Charm
Session 4	Jesus Prays in the Garden (Matthew 26:36-46)	I can pray!	• Philippians 4:13 • The Journey • This Is What I Pray • Jump Up! Walk a Little	• Diamond Art Suncatcher • Flip Book • Ribbon Paper Wreath
Session 5	Peter and John at the Temple (Acts 3:1-10)	I can hope!	• Snowball Mountain Challenge • C-O-U-R-A-G-E • Jump Up! Walk a Little • The Journey	• Challenge Medal • Cocoa Mug Frame • Scroll Paper Art • Tissue Paper Stars

Decorating Guide

100+ essential decorating ideas and how-tos!

Decorating Guide

Cokesbury Editorial/Design Team
Megan Ranjit .... Development Editor
Pamela Crosby .... Production Editor
Keitha Vincent .... Production and Design Manager
Micah Kandros .... Logo Design

Cokesbury Administrative Team
Brian K. Milford.................... President and Publisher
Marjorie M. Pon .... Associate Publisher and Editor, Church School Publications
Scott Spradley.................... Director and Editor, VBS
Heather Wegenka.................... Business Manager
Karla Taylor.................... Marketing Manager

Consulting and Production Team
Andy Wilson .... Songwriter and Producer
B4Entertainment.................... Video Producer
Adelicia Company .... Video Producer

Thank you to our consultant team! VBS 2026 Contributors, Reviewers, Testers, and Focus Group Members:

Our Team:
Keitha Vincent, Matt Allison (Development Assistance), Megan Ranjit, Selena Cunningham, Jonathan Higdon, Sarah Gregory, Scott Spradley, Karla Taylor (Marketing), Hank Hayes (Marketing), Dakota Rimmer (Marketing), Heather Wegenka (Business Manager)

Test Churches:
A&M United Methodist Church, College Station, TX; Connell Memorial United Methodist Church, Goodlettsville, TN; Heritage Presbyterian Church, Mason, OH; Zion Lutheran Church, Tamaqua, PA

Reviewers and Focus Group Members:
Michael Haspe, Tamaqua, PA; Amy Jo Alspaugh, Charlotte, NC; Rebecca Dyck, Chapel Hill, NC; Mallory Anderson, Lebanon, TN; Susie Faas, Mason, OH; Jenn Huff, Bloomington, IN; Susan Midkiff, Show Low, AZ; Salley Millsap, Murfreesboro, TN; Caitlin Bookwalter, Ormond Beach, FL; Lauren Bedevian; Houston, TX; Amy Perry, Burlington, VT; Becky Betz, Sugarland, TX; Kelsey Sledge, Cookeville, TN; David Barton, Goodlettsville, TN; Alayna Barton Peters, Goodlettsville, TN; Ashlea Barton, Goodlettsville, TN; Savannah Salas, College Station, TX; Mimi Sanders, Tucker, GA; Becci Benson, Enterprise, AL; Laurie Hembree, League City, TX; Lisa Kutinac, League City, TX; Andrea Jenkins, Virginia Beach, VA; Jan Russell, Minneapolis; MN, Amy Takahashi, Raleigh, NC; Brooke Wong, White House, TN; Charlotte Trafton, Austin, TX; Hannah Pratt, Murfreesboro, TN; Jayne´Kirk, Hurricane, WV; Jamie Muller, Tucker, GA; Kacie Jumper, Temple, TX; Lori Grasty, Elkhart, IN; Liz Greenban, Lake Arrowhead, CA; Laura Stinnett, Humble, TX; Sue Nieman, Lambertville, MI; Tiffany McClure, John's Creek, GA; Tiffany Barton, Goodlettsville, TN

Cokesbury VBS 2026
Snowball Mountain Challenge
Find Your Strength in God
Decorating Guide

ISBN: 9781791037604

Published by Abingdon Press, 810 12th Avenue South, Nashville, TN 37203. This leader book is part of Cokesbury's ***Snowball Mountain Challenge***

If you have questions or comments about using this resource, call 800-672-1789, a toll-free service available Monday through Friday from 8:00 to 4:00 Central Time. Calls at other times are recorded for response the next working day.

Two convenient ways to order in the U.S.: call 800-672-1789 or visit CokesburyVBS.com.

To place an order in Canada, call 800-265-6397 or email info@afcanada.com.

I can do all things through him who strengthens me. (Philippians 4:13, NRSV)

Science	Recreation	Snacks	Notes
• Straw Lift • Homemade Gummy Candy	• Laundry Basket Bobsled Race • Freezing Dreams Tag • Icy Mountain Motto Challenge	• Snowflakes • Snowflake Cupcakes • I Can Share My Gifts!	
• Instant Freeze • Blubber Glove	• Bible Verse Snowball Fling • Winter Clothes Race • Snow Queen/King Contest	• Snow-Drizzled Treats • Donut Snowman • I Can Be Brave!	
• Ball Bearing Ice • Notebook Tension	• Widow's Offering Hockey • Challengers' Slalom Race • Footprints in the Snow	• Hot Chocolate Mix • Snowman Pudding • I Can Give My All!	
• Coding Journey • Instant Snow	• Carry-for-Others Sled • Ice Skating Spin • Crawl and Waddle	• Snow Cream Dip • Ollie • I Can Pray!	
• Snowshoe Mountain Challenge • Soda Explosion	• Ski Lift Limbo • Cross-Country Skiing • Gold or Silver? NO!	• Snow-Covered Popcorn • Winter Sports • I Can Hope!	

Decorating Made Easy

Welcome to the Snowball Mountain Challenge Decorating Guide!

This guide is designed to help you transform your space in an exciting way that sparks the imaginations of kids and adults alike! Our goal at Cokesbury Kids VBS is to provide you with easy, attainable, and affordable decorating ideas that will wow your VBS participants and volunteers. Many of the ideas in this book can be completed with simple supplies that you may already have on hand in your supply closet, or that can be easily acquired at a local craft or hardware store. We want decorating to be easy so that your awesome volunteers can focus on the heart of VBS—sharing God's love with all who walk through the doors!

Along with this guide, we offer several other tools to help you plan and decorate with ease. Be sure to check out the following resources:

Snowball Mountain Challenge Director Guide

Work with your VBS Director to plan out all the important areas that need to be decorated. Make sure you are aware of the schedule, number of groups, and number of children participating in your VBS, as these numbers may affect your decorating decisions. You may wish to incorporate group names or other theme elements in your decorating.

Decorating and Publicity Download Files

Your **Snowball Mountain Challenge Kit**, either the **Ultimate Starter Kit** or **Digital Access Kit,** comes with a card that includes a link to digital downloads. Within these files is a Decorating and Publicity folder that contains clip art, images, and more that you may use to decorate your space. All items may be printed and copied for local church use only. Copyright 2026, Cokesbury Kids.

Decorating Video

Available for download on CokesburyVBS.com, this video highlights all of our decorating products so you can see how they are used.

Cokesbury VBS Website and Free Resources

Be sure to check out our website for purchasing all decorating items. We also have several items available for download in our FREE Resources section. Visit CokesburyVBS.com.

Snowball Mountain Challenge Bible Storyteller

Work closely with your Bible Storytelling leader to enhance the concepts that Challengers will be learning at Snowball Mountain Challenge VBS. Explore the **Bible Storyteller** for more ideas about decorating for spiritual growth and learning.

Cokebury VBS Pinterest Page

Follow Cokesbury VBS on Pinterest for a plethora of VBS ideas. Our boards contain inspiration and more for all of our published VBS programs!

Cokebury VBS Community Group on Facebook

Our Facebook Community is the place to go for decorating ideas! Along with photo albums from our test churches, you can engage with other VBS leaders and get tons of inspiration!

Products That Enhance

Make decorating even easier with these ready-to-use tools!

- **Activity Center Signs & Publicity Pack**
- **Banner Stand**
- **Bible Story Poster Pack**
- **Decorating Wall Curtain**
- **Decorating Mural Package**
- **Decorating Mobiles**
- **Decorating Pack**
- **Decorating Poster Pack**
- **Decorating Transparencies and Clip Art** found in the **Decorating and Publicity Download Files**
- **Digital Wall Art and Puppet Stage**
- **Large Logo Poster**
- **Logo String Flags**
- **Outdoor Banner**
- **Snowflake Garland**
- **Welcome Banner**
- **Wall Background**
- **VBS Theme Banner Poly**
- **VBS Theme Banner X Stand Combo**
- **XL Character Poster** (Ollie the Arctic Seal)

All this and more available at CokesburyVBS.com.

Supplies are limited so order early!

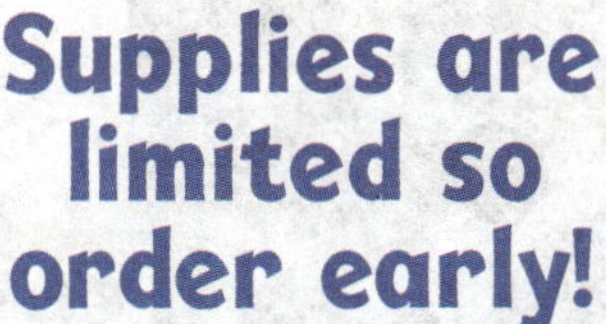

Welcome Challengers

Welcome to the Challenge

Choosing a central location for your welcome and registration/check-in area will bring the Snowball Mountain Challenge theme front and center when Challengers and volunteers enter your VBS. Here are a few tips to help your check-in/registration area pop:

- Begin displaying your **Snowball Mountain Challenge Outdoor Banner** several weeks in advance of your VBS.
- Equip your registration table with the **Snowball Mountain Challenge Tablecloths, Nametag Cards, Nametag Holders, VBS T-Shirts,** forms, pens, markers, and any other materials your team needs.
- Add more theme touches with the Ollie **XL Character Poster**, **Logo String Flags**, and more!
- Display your **VBS Theme Banner** to help introduce the key learnings (Lift Lessons) for the week.
- Hang the **Snowball Mountain Challenge Welcome Banner** in an eye-catching place.

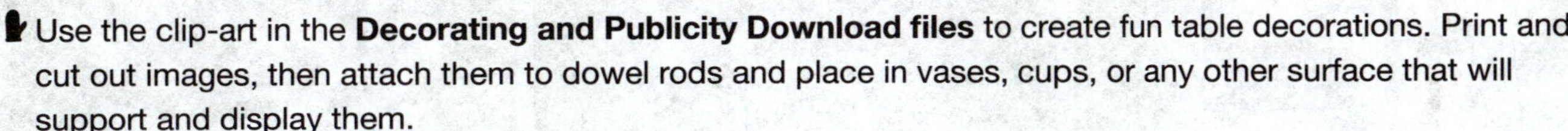

- Use the clip-art in the **Decorating and Publicity Download files** to create fun table decorations. Print and cut out images, then attach them to dowel rods and place in vases, cups, or any other surface that will support and display them.

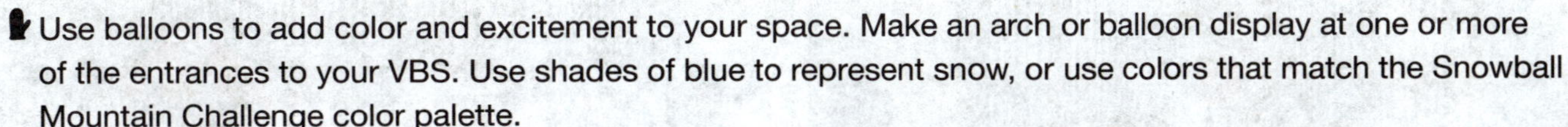

- Use balloons to add color and excitement to your space. Make an arch or balloon display at one or more of the entrances to your VBS. Use shades of blue to represent snow, or use colors that match the Snowball Mountain Challenge color palette.

Tip: The color palette, fonts, and logos can be found on the Snowball Mountain theme homepage at CokesburyVBS.com. Click on "Official Logo and Puppet." For detailed ink breakdowns and color references, see the Official Logo and Puppet File.

Font: Mingler family

Color palette:

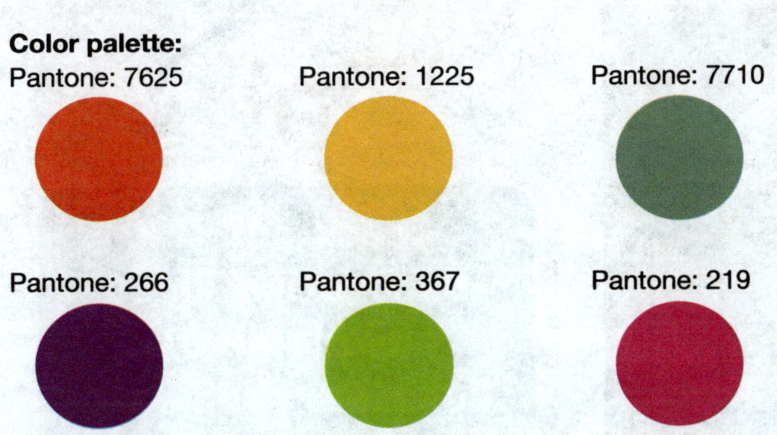

Pantone: 7625 Pantone: 1225 Pantone: 7710

Pantone: 266 Pantone: 367 Pantone: 219

Setting the Stage

Your assembly stage is where your Challengers will gather each day to hear from Ollie the Arctic Seal and their Activities Director (Assembly Leader), hear fun Snowball Mountain Challenge music, and get introduced to the Bible stories, Mountain Motto, and Lift Lessons.

- The **Decorating Murals** are a great option to bring your stage to life. Depending on your stage size and other decorating needs, you may purchase the **Decorating Mural,** the **Decorating Mural Extensions**, or the **Decorating Mural Package**, which includes both the main mural and the extensions. These murals can be attached to foam board, wood panels, or any other stand of your choice. Spray adhesive works great, but they can also be attached using tape, glue, or other adhesives.
- The center mural provides the focal point for your Assembly Time. The side murals complete the overall look and feel of Celebration Village area.

Decorating Mural – three panels to cover a 6' x 9' space
Decorating Mural Extension – six panels to cover a 6' x 18' space
Decorating Mural Package – nine panels to cover a 6' x 27' space

Check out the Decorating Video available at CokesburyVBS.com!

Setting the Stage

Here are a few decorating items to add to your stage. Many of these items may already be in your VBS closet or can easily be donated by your congregation:

- **Logo String Flags** for a fun competition feel
- White snow blankets to create a bottom layer of snow
- White polyfil to add more textured snow
- White craft styrofoam balls to mimic snowballs, various sizes
- Artificial pine trees
- Sleds, toboggans, skis, inner tubes, and other winter sports paraphernalia

The Challenge Board (page 10) and puppet stage (page 11) serve as integral parts of Assembly Time. The puppet stage can be designed to be Ollie's live stream set-up as he/she reports on the Snowball Mountain Challenge. Each day, Challengers will search for a challenge medal to bring back to the stage to display on the Challenge Board. See the **Assembly Leader** for more information if you plan on incorporating these items.

Challenge Board

Each day's Lift Lesson (key learning) will be reinforced on the Challenge Board that you create for your assembly area. Here is just one idea on how to create the board, as well as the Challenge medals that Challengers will find/earn each day. Read through the **Assembly Leader** for more details.

Materials and Instructions

- **Decorating Mobiles**
- **Decorating Poster Pack**
- **Snowflake Garland**
- Large piece of foam insulation board (approximately 5' by 3')
- Pre-cut letters
- Spray adhesive or hot glue gun and glue
- Large craft paper
- Extra-large push pins or dowel rods
- Thick ribbon in various colors
- Single-hole punch
- Scissors
- Spray paint (optional)

1. Use spray adhesive or hot glue to cover a large piece of foam board with craft paper. Alternatively, you may wish to spray paint your board.
2. Place five large push-pins or dowel rods (something the medals can hang on) on the board, equally spaced apart. Be sure to leave room for the medals to comfortably hang. Attach the pins or rods to the board using hot glue. You may also choose to use a drill to create holes and secure the pins or rods on the back of the board.
3. Use pre-cut out letters to title your Challenge Board.
4. Decorate your board with the **Snowflake Garland**, posters from the **Decorating Poster Pack**, polyfil, or anything else you wish.
5. To create the medals, simply punch a hole in each of the five Lift Lesson posters from the **Decorating Mobiles**. Cut ribbon into approximately 14" pieces, or however long is needed for the medals to comfortably hang on the board. Thread the ribbon through the hole and tie a knot. Rotate the ribbon so that the knot is hidden in the back.

Ollie's Puppet Stage

Our lovable puppet, Ollie, has traveled to Snowball Mountain to report live on the challenge, and the puppet stage will help display him/her in a fun and engaging way. There are many ways to set up a puppet stage, depending on your space and stage size.

If you are able, use the following instructions to create a larger-than-life puppet stage for Ollie. If your space is limited, be sure to check out our **Cokebury VBS Community Facebook Group** and **Cokesbury VBS Pinterest Page** for more pictures and ideas of how you can execute a puppet stage for Ollie the Arctic Seal.

Materials and Instructions

- **Puppet Stage** wrap from the **Snowball Mountain Challenge Digital Wall Art & Puppet Stage**
- **Large Logo Poster**
- **Decorating Poster Pack**
- **Wall Background**
- Three 4' by 8' pieces of foam insulation board (to be cut down to 4' by 7')
- Precision craft knife or hot knife
- Spray adhesive or hot glue gun and glue
- Duct tape

1. Download and print the **Puppet Stage Wrap** from CokesburyVBS.com. We recommend printing at a local print shop that can handle large-scale projects.
2. Use a precision craft knife to cut out a window on one of the boards. The window should be approximately 2' wide by 1' tall.
3. Use hot glue or spray adhesive to attach the wrap to each piece of the foam board. Trim the foam board to match the size of the puppet wrap (4' by 7'). Make sure to cut out a window for the puppet's position.
4. Cut a piece of the **Wall Background** to make a curtain for the window. Attach the curtain to the back of the board using hot glue or other adhesive.
5. Use duct tape to attach the three pieces of the stage together. Lay the boards on a flat surface and tape from behind. Make sure the taped seams are able to bend so the puppet stage can stand alone and upright.
6. For more color, add the **Large Logo Poster** or posters from the **Decorating Poster Pack** to the puppet stage.

Enhance Your Hallways

Sky-High Ski Lift

The best way to experience all that Snowball Mountain has to offer is on a ski lift! Many people enjoy bringing out their collection of puppets from VBS programs of years past to incorporate them in the decorating. A ski lift is a great way to have your puppet friends engage in the Snowball Mountain fun. If you don't have a collection of puppets to use other beloved stuffed animals, pictures of your Challengers, or simply create a fun ski lift for aesthetic purposes.

Materials and Instructions

- Previous Cokesbury VBS puppets or other stuffed animals
- Rope
- Plastic lawn chairs (child-sized Adirondack style) or wood slats
- Electric drill
- Adhesive hooks (optional)

1. Using an electric drill, create four holes through each chair of your ski lift. You should have a hole on each side of the chair, one at the top and one at the bottom.
2. Thread rope through all four holes of each chair, linking all the chairs together.
3. Secure the ski lift to the wall (or object) in your desired space. If you do not have something to safely secure your ski lift to, consider using adhesive hooks that can hold the weight of your chairs and puppets. (This will vary depending on how many chairs and puppets you choose to display.)

Snow-Covered Trees and Mountains

One of the easiest ways to enhance your hallways is with snow-covered trees and mountains. Invite volunteers to help you make as many trees and mountains as possible, in various sizes, to place throughout your hallways and spaces.

Materials and Instructions

- **Clip Art** from the **Decorating and Publicity Download files**
- **Snowflake Garland (optional)**
- Projector
- Pencils
- Large pieces of cardboard
- Precision craft knife or strong scissors
- Green paint
- Gray or brown paint
- White paint
- Aerosol snow spray (optional)

1. From the clip art files, select a tree or mountain image and project it onto a large piece of cardboard. Trace the tree and cut out.
2. Paint the mountains gray or brown, and paint the trees green.
3. Use white paint to add the look of snow to your trees and mountains.
4. For more depth, add textured snow to your trees and mountains by spraying aerosol snow to the white-painted portions.
5. Add falling snowflakes on your mountains and trees. Cut apart a **Snowflake Garland**, or print out snowflakes from the **Decorating and Publicity Download files**.

Snowy Slopes

Showcase the reason we are all here at Snowball Mountain Challenge—to hit the slopes! Highlight a variety of winter sports fun by turning your hallways into the snowy banks and slopes of Snowball Mountain.

Materials and Instructions

- **Clip Art** from the **Decorating and Publicity Download Files**
- **Snowflake Garland** (optional)
- **Logo String Flags** (optional)
- Projector
- Pencil
- Large craft paper in various colors such as blue, white, and purple (The amount of craft paper will be determined by the hallway length and space you plan to cover.)
- Scissors
- Blue painter's tape, spray adhesive, or other adhesive of your choice

1. Cover the top half of your wall with blue craft paper.
2. On a large piece of white craft paper, trace curved lines to represent a snowbank. Use scissors to cut out the snowbank pieces.
3. Adhere the white craft paper, representing the snowbank, to the blue paper.
4. Use a projector to trace clip art images of winter sports kids in action from the **Decorating and Publicity Download Files**. Use a variety of colors and sports.
5. Strategically place the winter sports kids along the snowbanks/slopes to showcase the Snowball Mountain Challenge fun.

Tablecloth Tents

Many of us have been to a fun event where there are tents galore! Add tablecloth tents to the walls in your spaces to bring the challenge excitement to your Challengers. This is a simple way to make your space feel like a winter sports event. Use the tents to showcase different scenes (as shown below) or simply have colorful tents placed throughout your space.

Materials and Instructions

- **Logo String Flags**
- Plastic tablecloths in a variety of colors (at least 8 per tent)
- Long and tall cardboard boxes
- Tape or other adhesive

1. Using a cardboard box approximately 7' tall (or stacking several boxes on top of one another), create a 3' frame (approximate) for your tent, extending from the wall. Cover the boxes with plastic tablecloths and secure.
2. Hang plastic tablecloths on the wall to create the back of the tent.
3. Gather 2–3 tablecloths into a point, secure the points with tape, and then drape them above the cardboard box frame to create the top part of the tent.
4. Enclose the tent by draping a tablecloth on each side.
5. Decorate the front of the tent with **Logo String Flags.**

Ready-Made Hallway Options

We have two great options for simply adding dimension, texture, and excitement to your hallways. If you have a wall that you aren't quite sure what to do with, use our ready-made options! All you have to do is hang them on the wall and your space is automatically transformed! The iridescent **Decorating Curtain** and snowflake **Wall Background** can be used almost anywhere. We recommend adding the **Decorating Curtain** on top of brightly colored paper for an even more exciting look. Strategically place posters from the **Decorating Poster Pack**, images from the **Decorating Pack**, or clip art images from the **Decorating and Publicity Download Files** to emphasize what the Challengers will be learning throughout the week.

Bible Stories Come Alive

Your hallways are a great place to help Challengers remember the Bible stories they will be hearing each day. With simple supplies like craft paper and markers, you can create biblical scenes to help bring the Bible stories to life. Below are a few examples to spark ideas.

Session 1 – Joseph Interprets Dreams
Session 2 – Esther Shows Courage
Session 3 – The Widow's Offering
Session 4 – Jesus Prays in the Garden
Session 5 – Peter and John at the Temple

SNOW TUBE
BOOGIE

SNOWBALL
MOUNTAIN
CHALLENGE

Boys
Bathroom

Girls
Bathroom

Make Your Stations Shine

Creative Signage

A great VBS includes attractive, helpful signs that show Challengers and volunteers where to go. Be sure to check out the **Activity Center Sings and Publicity Pack** for a variety of station signs and other versatile signs that can be used to provide directions and add a splash of fun to your stations and hallways. Once inside your stations, remind Challengers of the Lift Lessons and the Mountain Motto by displaying items from the **Decorating Pack** and posters from the **Decorating Poster Pack**. Consider hanging the **Decorating Mobiles** from the ceilings of your station rooms.

Create signs for your stations, giving each area a creative theme name. Below are some ideas to get you started.

Large Challenge Medals

Challenge Medals play an important role in Snowball Mountain Challenge VBS, and you may wish to use them as large decorating devices to help reinforce key learnings throughout your VBS.

Materials and Instructions

- **Clip Art** from the **Decorating and Publicity Download files**
- Projector
- Pencil
- Precision craft knife or scissors
- Large pieces of cardboard, at least five (one for each daily lift lesson)
- Acrylic paint in various colors
- Paintbrushes or sponges
- Letter stencils (optional)

1. Project the medal clip art from the **Decorating and Publicity Download Files** on to a large piece of cardboard and trace.
2. Use a knife or scissors to cut out the medal.
3. Paint the medal in your desired colors.
4. Use letter stencils (or freehand drawing) to add the daily Lift Lessons: I can share my gifts! I can be brave! I can give my all! I can pray! I can hope!
5. Optional: make a medal to display the Mountain Motto.
6. Display the medals in eye-catching places.

Storytelling Backdrops

Your Bible storytelling room is a great place to tie in theme-specific decorations as Challengers meet together to hear the Bible story of the day. Transform your Bible storytelling space into a cozy ski lodge room complete with a fireplace (artificial) and comfy, warm furnishings, or display an outdoor winter scene to invoke gathering together outside.

Another option for your Bible storytelling room is to use biblical backdrops that work for multiple days. We especially recommend this option if you are choosing to use Storytelling Option 1 (drama). As shown below, consider an indoor palace/temple backdrop for Day 1 (Joseph Interprets Dreams), Day 2 (Esther Shows Courage), Day 3 (The Widow's Offering), and Day 5 (Peter and John at the Temple). An outdoor garden scene can be used for Day 4 (Jesus Prays in the Garden).

Add other items to your Bible storytelling room such as artificial plants and trees, pillows for sitting, benches, and more.

Encourage Spiritual Growth

Spiritual Growth Decorating Ideas

- Create a special space designated for prayer, shown as a Prayer Chalet below.
- Have a response wall for Challengers to share what they have learned throughout the week. Use **Clip Art** from the **Decorating and Publicity Download Files** to decorate the wall, and include prompts that encourage Challengers to respond to the Lift Lessons each day, or with their prayer requests.
- Create a missions bulletin board or wall to remind Challengers of your mission project for the week.

What ideas do you have? Share your ideas in our Cokebury VBS Community Facebook group!

Decorating Donations Checklist

- ❏ Skis
- ❏ Inner tubes or snow tubes
- ❏ Sleds
- ❏ Toboggans
- ❏ Ice skates
- ❏ Ice hockey sticks
- ❏ Artificial pine trees
- ❏ White snow blankets
- ❏ Winter hats
- ❏ Winter gloves
- ❏ Ski jackets
- ❏ Ski goggles
- ❏ Scarves
- ❏ Styrofoam balls in various sizes to make snowballs
- ❏ Cardboard boxes in various shapes and sizes
- ❏ Plastic tablecloths in various colors
- ❏ Artificial snow
- ❏ Polyfil
- ❏ ______________________________
- ❏ ______________________________
- ❏ ______________________________
- ❏ ______________________________
- ❏ ______________________________

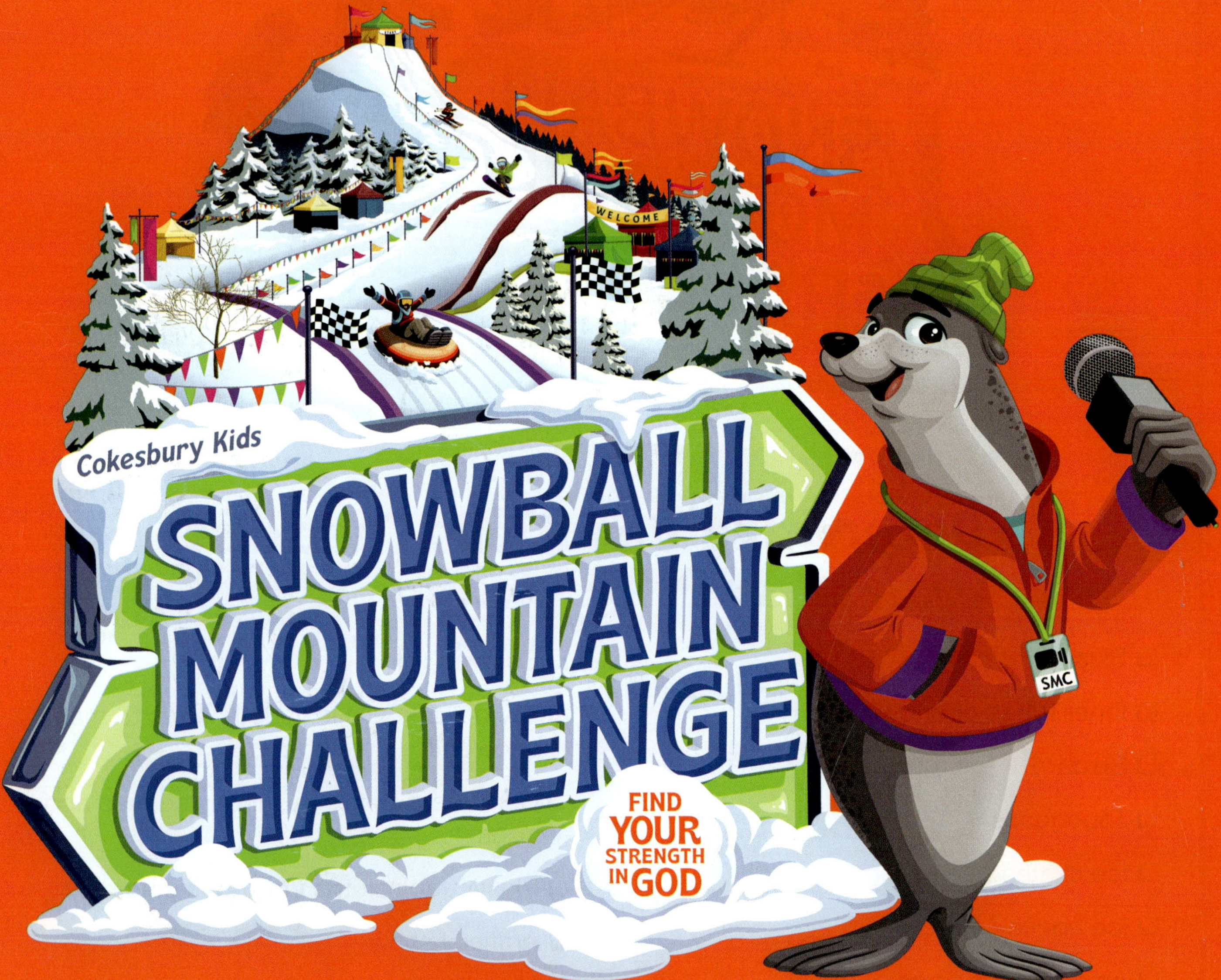

Cokesbury Kids

SNOWBALL MOUNTAIN CHALLENGE

FIND YOUR STRENGTH IN GOD

www.cokesburykids.com

RELIGION/Christian Education/Children & Youth

ISBN-13: 978-1-7910-3760-4